CW01513073

Astron

Written by

John Dougherty

Illustrated by

Louise Pigott

OXFORD
UNIVERSITY PRESS

OXFORD
UNIVERSITY PRESS

Great Clarendon Street, Oxford, OX2 6DP, United Kingdom

Oxford University Press is a department of the University of Oxford.
It furthers the University's objective of excellence in research, scholarship,
and education by publishing worldwide. Oxford is a registered trade mark
of Oxford University Press in the UK and in certain other countries

Text © John Dougherty 2015
Illustrations © Louise Pigott 2015

The moral rights of the author have been asserted

First published 2015

All rights reserved. No part of this publication may
be reproduced, stored in a retrieval system, or transmitted,
in any form or by any means, without the prior permission in
writing of Oxford University Press, or as expressly permitted
by law, by licence or under terms agreed with the appropriate
reprographics rights organization. Enquiries concerning
reproduction outside the scope of the above should be sent to the
Rights Department, Oxford University Press, at the address above.

You must not circulate this work in any other form
and you must impose this same condition on any acquirer

British Library Cataloguing in Publication Data
Data available

ISBN: 978-0-19-835647-9

10 9 8 7 6 5 4 3 2 1

Paper used in the production of this book is a natural, recyclable product
made from wood grown in sustainable forests. The manufacturing process
conforms to the environmental regulations of the country of origin.

Printed in China by Hing Yip

Acknowledgements

Series Advisor: Nikki Gamble

Astron and his family lived in space.
One day they had to make a long journey.
Space felt huge and cold to Astron.

He stayed close to his parents.

Suddenly, there was a meteor storm.
A meteor came too close and Astron
lost his parents. He was terrified.
The meteors were everywhere!

Astron called for his parents but he could
not find them. The storm went on for hours.

When the meteor storm was over, Astron was alone. He was lost in the blackness of space. He drifted sadly in the dark.

Then Astron saw a strange thing. He started to fly towards it.

Astron had never seen a thing like this before. It was made of metal.

There were creatures *inside* it! He could see one of the creatures looking out.

The creature inside could see him, too.

The creature looked very strange to Astron.
It did not glow. It had no wings.

It did not even have a thought-web.
How can it talk without a thought-web?
Astron wondered.

Astron used his thought-web to listen to the creature's thoughts. Astron could tell that she was good and kind. Her name was Olivia and she was on a spaceship. She thought Astron was very strange but very beautiful.

Astron used his thought-web again. He told Olivia what he was thinking. He told her that he was lost and he needed to find his parents.

Olivia's eyes widened.

She called out to her parents. Now Astron could see how Olivia talked.

Olivia told her parents that Astron was lost. But her parents were scared of Astron and they would not listen. Olivia was cross with them.

Olivia's parents ran to the
controls of the spaceship.
They wanted to get away from
Astron as fast as possible.

The spaceship disappeared between the stars.

Using his thought-web, Astron felt Olivia's sadness deep inside. He cried.

Suddenly, Astron could feel that Olivia was afraid. He listened to Olivia's thoughts. Something bad was happening to her!

Fierce creatures called dark-biters were around the spaceship.

The dark-biters were hungry and cruel.
They were going to eat the spaceship.
Olivia and her parents were in danger!

Astron had to save Olivia. He stretched
out his wings as **wide** as they would go.
He flew faster than he had ever flown before.
Astron hoped he would get to
Olivia in time.

Soon Astron saw the spaceship. He was tired but he flew even faster.

The dark-biters were nibbling at the spaceship now.
Olivia was in great danger!
Astron went faster. He glowed **brighter**.

Then **brighter** still.

By the time Astron reached the spaceship,
he was shining with a very bright light.
The dark-biters were afraid of Astron's light.
They moved away from the spaceship.
Astron shone **brighter**
and brighter,
and the dark-biters fled.

When the dark-biters had gone, Astron
had no strength left. His light began to fade.
His wings folded. Everything seemed far away.

He closed his eyes and
drifted off into space,
alone and cold.

Someone took hold of Astron.
It was Olivia's mother. She took
him into the spaceship.

Olivia was upset. "We have to help him!" she cried. "We will help him," said Olivia's father. "I'm sorry we were afraid of him."

Olivia's mother said, "Maybe we can find out where his family is. Let's use the computer to look."

After a while, the computer beeped. Had it found Astron's family?

The spaceship flew towards the signal.

Soon, Astron could hear his family's thoughts. He felt a warm glow of happiness as he got closer to his family.

Olivia opened the spaceship door. She cried as she said goodbye to Astron.

Astron cried, too. He might never see Olivia again but he knew they would always be friends.

Astron flew through the door and went to join his parents.

As the spaceship flew away, Astron
saw Olivia waving. He stretched out his
wings and waved back.

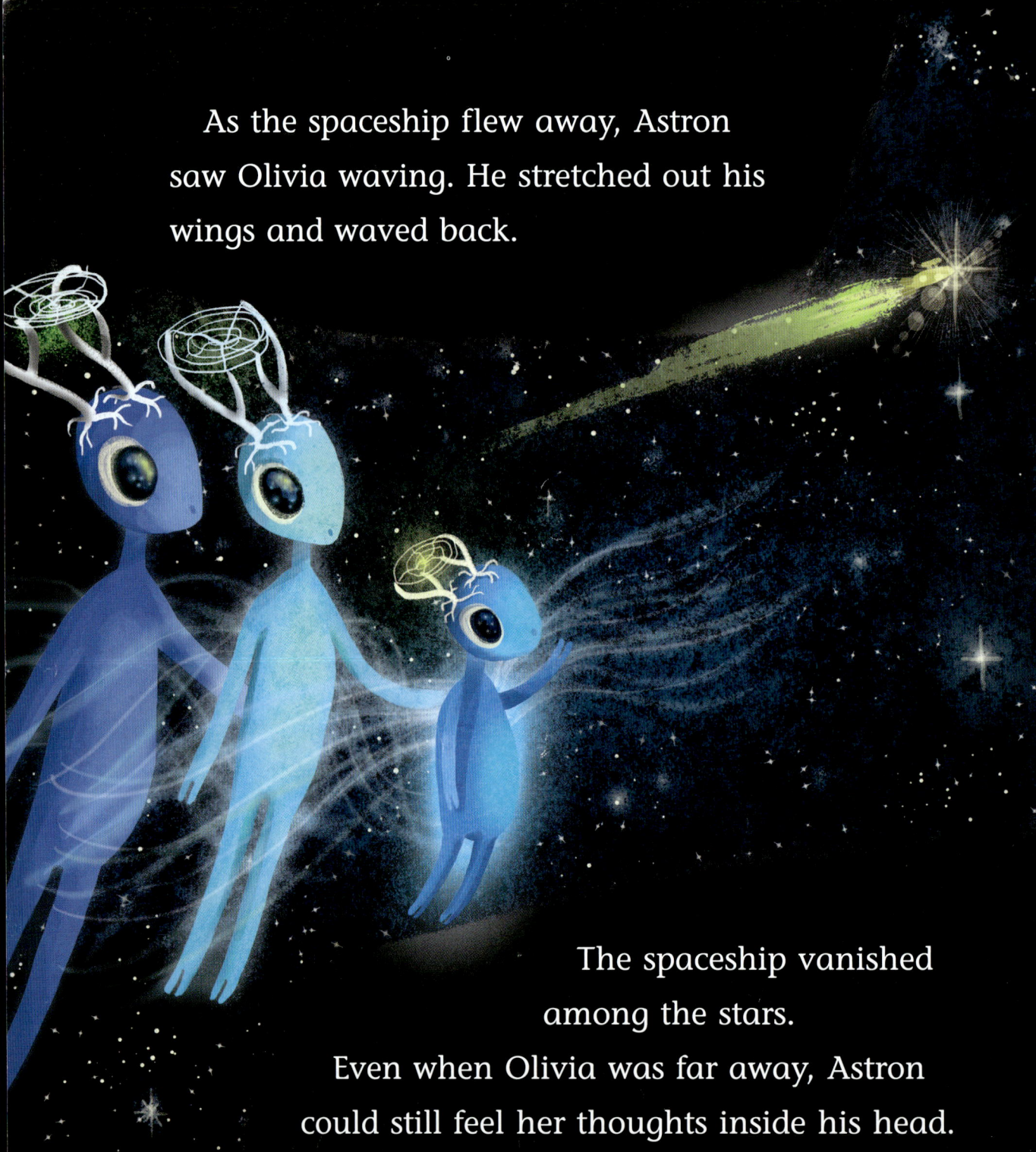

The spaceship vanished
among the stars.
Even when Olivia was far away, Astron
could still feel her thoughts inside his head.